THE AMAZING STORY OF
NOAH'S ARK

Written and illustrated by
Marcia Williams

WALKER BOOKS
AND SUBSIDIARIES
LONDON · BOSTON · SYDNEY

Many, many summers

and winters ago,

God became angry with the world

because people had become so cruel.

They were stealing and lying,

cheating and fighting,

so God decided to destroy them all.

Everyone except for Noah and his family.

For Noah was a good, kind man.

"Noah," said God, "I will save all your family

and a male and female of every animal.

The rest will drown in a fearful flood."

"Build a great ark of cypress wood,

with a door and a window.
Build it three storeys high
and fill it with food."

Noah and his family worked hard building the ark.

They chopped down trees

and sawed the logs.

They hammered the wood

and covered it with pitch.

Other people pointed their fingers

and laughed at Noah.

They thought he was mad

talking of floods and building an ark.

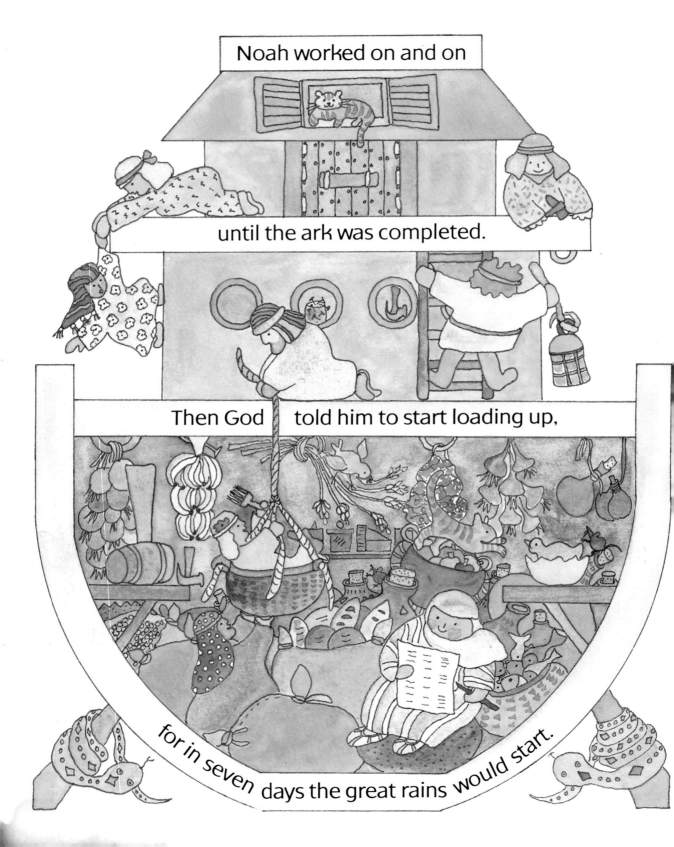

Noah worked on and on

until the ark was completed.

Then God told him to start loading up,

for in seven days the great rains would start.

Noah thought he might have trouble catching all the animals. But he didn't, for God had told them to go to Noah and climb aboard his ark.

The animals went in two by two –

giraffes and birds and elephants,

bears and sheep and spotted monsters,

lions and seals, zebras and snakes,

walruses, guinea fowl and pigs, and

WELCO

rhinos and camels and ladybirds,

leopards and rabbits and unicorns,

a cow and bull and a pair of goats,

all the tiny insects which Noah could hardly see.

It was hard work squeezing them all in!

But when the first drops of rain fell,

the last insect found a bed

and the great doors were slammed shut.

For forty days and forty nights the rain fell.

The ark was lifted above the earth.

The waters rose higher and higher

until even the tallest mountain was covered.

Not a creature on earth was left alive.

And still it rained on and on.

For many days the ark drifted.

Then God sent a wind over the earth, and

down

down

down

the waters went.

Finally,

after seven long months,

the ark came to rest on Mount Ararat.

Noah opened the window and let out a raven.

But it could find nowhere to land.

Noah opened
the window again

and sent out a dove.

It flew far and wide

but could find nowhere
to rest.

Seven days later

Noah sent out the
dove once more.

In the evening it returned
to the ark.

In its beak it carried
an olive branch.

This told Noah that soon
the waters would dry.

He pushed open the great door.

Out rushed Noah's family and all the animals,
joyful to walk on land again.

Noah built an altar to thank God.

God was so pleased that He promised Noah

never to flood the world again.

A rainbow appeared as a sign of His promise.

Noah was very happy to see this.

He made a new home and planted a vineyard

and lived to a very great age

with his family and all the creatures of the ark

and their many children.

So now, whenever it rains and you see a rainbow,

you can remember the story of Noah.

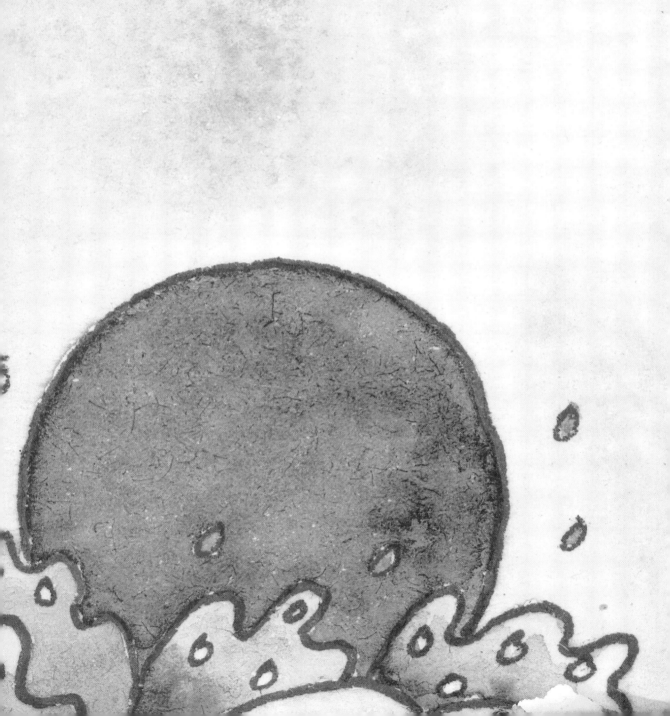

MORE WALKER PAPERBACKS
For You to Enjoy

Other retellings by Marcia Williams

JONAH AND THE WHALE

When Jonah disobeys God, he finds himself in the belly of an enormous whale!
More comic-strip Bible story fun.

"What makes Marcia Williams' version of the story so absorbing are the
wonderfully detailed and beautiful illustrations…
A picture book full of life and colour." *Child Education*

0-7445-6059-4　£4.99

JOSEPH AND HIS MAGNIFICENT COAT OF MANY COLOURS

Full of drama, incident and emotion, the adventures of Joseph are as
colourful as his glorious coat itself.

"Every page is awash with colour and detail…
Children will find much to enjoy here." *Child Education*

0-7445-6060-8　£4.99

THE ILIAD AND THE ODYSSEY

The Iliad tells the story of the war between the Greeks and the Trojans.
The Odyssey depicts the perilous voyage home of the Greek warrior, Odysseus.

"A big, beautifully produced book, telling the stories in irresistibly detailed
comic-strip form… Elegant, intelligent, funny, dramatic and totally absorbing;
the perfect start to an early familiarity with Homer." *The Guardian*

0-7445-5430-6　£5.99

Walker Paperbacks are available from most booksellers, or by post from B.B.C.S., P.O. Box 941, Hull, North Humberside HU1 3YQ
24 hour telephone credit card line 01482 224626

To order, send: Title, author, ISBN number and price for each book ordered, your full name and address,
cheque or postal order payable to BBCS for the total amount and allow the following for postage and packing:
UK and BFPO: £1.00 for the first book, and 50p for each additional book to a maximum of £3.50.
Overseas and Eire: £2.00 for the first book, £1.00 for the second and 50p for each additional book.

Prices and availability are subject to change without notice.